# Sally Comet and the Space Pirates

St Georges C of E Foundation
School Primary Phase
Westwood Road
Broadstairs

Level 9 – Gold

# Helpful Hints for Reading at Home

The graphemes (written letters) and phonemes (units of sound) used throughout this series are aligned with Letters and Sounds. This offers a consistent approach to learning whether reading at home or in the classroom.

HERE ARE SOME COMMON WORDS THAT YOUR CHILD MIGHT FIND TRICKY:

| water | where | would | know | thought | through | couldn't |
| laughed | eyes | once | we're | school | can't | our |

## TOP TIPS FOR HELPING YOUR CHILD TO READ:

- Encourage your child to read aloud as well as silently to themselves.
- Allow your child time to absorb the text and make comments.
- Ask simple questions about the text to assess understanding.
- Encourage your child to clarify the meaning of new vocabulary.

This book focuses on developing independence, fluency and comprehension. It is a gold level 9 book band.

# Sally Comet
## and the
# Space Pirates

**Written by**
Robin Twiddy

**Illustrated by**
Richard Bayley

Hi, my name is Sally Comet and I live with my parents on the famous spaceship The Gold-Wing. Mum and Dad are archaeologists.

They fly all around the galaxy looking for ancient treasures and forgotten things. Whatever they find ends up in the planet-sized museum Historia, and I get to go with them wherever they go.

It is great! I get to meet so many special and unique people and I always learn something amazing. There was the time we met the wandering people on the planet Tartus. They taught me lots of great songs and how to throw my voice so that it sounds like I am in a different room. So cool!

And of course, there were the lizard people of Cormac 5. They taught me how to move like a shadow, silent and invisible. Yes, every day on The Gold-Wing is an adventure, but some adventures are bigger than others.

However, the adventure that I really want to tell you about is the time that I outsmarted the meanest space pirates in the whole galaxy. It all began on the planet Tarth. Mum and Dad had just finished exploring the tomb of the ancient pharaoh Varden Kar the Third.

We had loaded all the treasures into the cargo hold. There was the golden sarcophagus of the pharaoh (with a real-life mummy inside!), a sceptre decorated with glimmering jewels, and bags and bags of coins and knick-knacks. Dad said it was the best find ever!

Once everything had been loaded, we blasted off and set a course for the museum. Normally, travelling back to the museum was the most boring part, but not this time. We had only been travelling for a day when we received a distress call. Dad punched the call up onto the screen in the cockpit.

"Oh, thank Gorban. Finally, someone has found us. Our ship broke down and we had to land on this planet. Please help!" said the figure in the middle. There was something about him that I just didn't trust. Maybe it was all his missing teeth or the two eye patches, or maybe it was the laser-hook hand or even the peg leg. Something just didn't add up.

"Sally, your mum and I have to help these nice men. I want you to stay here and do your homework. We won't be long," said Dad. "Send over your coordinates," Mum said to the shadowy figure. "We will be right there. I'm a pretty good engineer, we will have you up and running in no time at all."

We followed the coordinates to a small and gloomy swamp planet. The Gold-Wing landed near to a large and shabby ship. It was really beaten up and covered in branches and slime from the swamp. Mum and Dad grabbed their tools and disappeared into the mists, heading towards the other ship. It was then that I decided to follow them.

When Mum and Dad arrived, they were invited inside. I got closer to the ship to investigate. I pulled one of the branches leaning on the ship. It fell loose and I made a shocking discovery. A Jolly Roger! "Pirates!" I gasped. "I was right!" Mum and Dad were in some serious trouble. Just then, I heard boots clanking on metal. The sound was getting closer. I hid.

"Argh, they didn't suspect a thing," said the tall and wobbly pirate. He looked like someone had thrown an old hat on a giant pink jelly. "You are so smart, Captain, luring them in with a distress call. Now they are fixing our ship and we can rob them."

"You are right, Slithe. I am very clever," said the big one with the eye patches, peg leg and laser-hook hand, now grinning a big ugly grin. "Now, let's go and get all that booty we saw them load onto their ship. We're going to be rich!"

It was then that I knew that it was up to me to stop them!

When I got back to The Gold-Wing, I found the pirates trying to break into the cargo hold. I knew it would take them a while to get through – just enough time to put my plan into action.

First, I ran to the storeroom where we kept all our equipment for our digs. I grabbed the tablet computer and filled a bag with some really thin wires and the standing lights that Mum and Dad use on their digs. Once I had everything, I slipped into the cargo bay through an air vent.

When they finally broke in, I was waiting, silent like a shadow. "Ay, look at all this booty, boys," shouted the captain. The third pirate, who appeared to be made from moss or some other type of plant, started dancing and tossing golden coins and jewels in the air.

"Quick, lads. Start filling your sacks," ordered the captain. It was time to put my plan into action. A few quick taps on the tablet computer and I was in control of the lights that I had set up earlier. In the shadows, I gripped the near-invisible strings and thought to myself: "It's now or never."

I flicked the first light on, and it shined straight into the pirates' eyes. Then I changed the shape of my throat, just how the travelling people on Tartus had taught me, and threw my voice.

"Who disturbs me?" came my voice from the other side of the room. It was much deeper than my normal voice. The travellers on Tartus had taught me that too. "Who seeks my treasure?" I added.

The pirates in the spotlight tried covering their eyes with their hands and spinning around trying to find where the voice was coming from.

"I am Boggle-Eye Bill," said the captain defiantly. "Captain of The Flying Dutchcan!"

Then I activated the next light. This one lit up the open sarcophagus of Pharaoh Varden Kar the Third. I pulled on the strings. They ran up from my hands, over some beams in the ceiling and down to the pharaoh's mummy where they were attached to his arms. I threw my voice again and pulled on the strings. The pharaoh seemed to come to life.

"Beware the curse of the pharaoh! Those who take my treasures will pay the price!" I made the pharaoh say, as the strings caused his arms to flail around threateningly.

"Arrrrrrrrrr, it's alive! The treasure is haunted! Let's get out of here!" shouted the jelly pirate, his whole body wobbling with fear.

"It's not worth it, boys! Back to the ship!" the captain screamed. He no longer sounded fierce or confident. In fact, his voice was shrill and high-pitched. And with that, the pirates fled to their ship. I followed to make sure that Mum and Dad were alright.

I had never seen adults run so fast. In seconds, they were back at their ship where Mum and Dad had just finished making the repairs. They were just then stepping out of The Flying Dutchcan.

"There we are," said Dad. "All fixed up and ready to go."

"It really wasn't that hard to fix," said Mum. "You should take better care of your ship if you don't want to end up stranded again." The pirates didn't even thank Mum and Dad. They just ran onto their ship and blasted straight into space.

"Ah, Sally, there you are," said Dad. "They were a strange bunch. I wonder what got into them."

"What have you been up to Sally?" Mum asked.

"Oh, nothing much," I replied.

And that is the story of how I, Sally Comet, outsmarted the space pirates, with a little help from Pharaoh Varden Kar the Third!

# Sally Comet and the Space Pirates

1. On what planet did Sally learn how to throw her voice?
   (a) Cormac 5
   (b) Pluto
   (c) Tartus

2. Sally realises that the call for help came from pirates when she discovered a Jolly Roger. What is a Jolly Roger?

3. How did Sally make it look like the mummy was moving?

4. What is the name of the pirates' ship?

5. Why do you think Sally didn't tell her parents about the pirates?

©2021 **BookLife Publishing Ltd.**
King's Lynn, Norfolk PE30 4LS

ISBN 978-1-83927-401-5

All rights reserved. Printed in Malaysia.
A catalogue record for this book is available from the British Library.

**Sally Comet and the Space Pirates**
Written by Robin Twiddy
Illustrated by Richard Bayley

# An Introduction to BookLife Readers...

Our Readers have been specifically created in line with the London Institute of Education's approach to book banding and are phonetically decodable and ordered to support each phase of Letters and Sounds.

Each book has been created to provide the best possible reading and learning experience. Our aim is to share our love of books with children, providing both emerging readers and prolific page-turners with beautiful books that are guaranteed to provoke interest and learning, regardless of ability.

**BOOK BAND GRADED** using the Institute of Education's approach to levelling.

**PHONETICALLY DECODABLE** supporting each phase of Letters and Sounds.

**EXERCISES AND QUESTIONS** to offer reinforcement and to ascertain comprehension.

**BEAUTIFULLY ILLUSTRATED** to inspire and provoke engagement, providing a variety of styles for the reader to enjoy whilst reading through the series.

AUTHOR INSIGHT:
**ROBIN TWIDDY**

Robin Twiddy is one of BookLife Publishing's most creative and prolific editorial talents, who imbues all his copy with a sense of adventure and energy. Robin's Cambridge-based first class honours degree in psychosocial studies offers a unique viewpoint on factual information and allows him to relay information in a manner that readers of any age are guaranteed to retain. He also holds a certificate in Teaching in the Lifelong Sector, and a postgraduate certificate in Consumer Psychology.

A father of two, Robin has written over 70 titles for BookLife and specialises in conceptual, role-playing narratives which promote interaction with the reader and inspire even the most reluctant of readers to fully engage with his books.

This book focuses on developing independence, fluency and comprehension. It is a gold level 9 book band.